(Silver Burdett Picture Histories)

Napoleon's Europe

Pierre Miquel
Illustrated by Jacques Poirier

Translated by Eva Krauss
from La Vie Privée des Hommes: Au temps de Napoléon
First published in France in 1979 by
Librairie Hachette, Paris

© Librairie Hachette, 1979. Adapted and published in the
United States by Silver Burdett Company, Morristown, N.J. 1983 Printing.

ISBN 0-382-06622-7
Library of Congress Catalog Card No. 81-52601

Contents

Europe under Napoleon

In 1789, not long after the American Revolution, the French people rose up against the old regime—the monarchy of Louis XVI and Marie Antoinette. The monarchy had become increasingly repressive and inefficient, and the French people wanted more freedom—and more influence over the way the government was run.

A succession of revolutionary governments wrote new constitutions and attempted to control domestic unrest and foreign intervention. But the governments were weak, and the problems remained. At times extremists controlled the government. One such time was during the Reign of Terror in 1793–94, when many people were sentenced to death on the guillotine. After years of unsettled government, the people were ready for a strong leader. In 1799 Napoleon Bonaparte, a successful army general, took advantage of this opportunity and assumed control of the government.

From the beginning of the French Revolution, the other monarchies of old Europe were uneasy. The czar of Russia, who reigned over a kingdom of serfs, and the emperor of Austria, who also had not abolished serfdom, marched thousands of men toward the French borders. The king of Prussia gave strong support to these armies, as did the king of Spain. The English ordered sea blockades. The Revolution seemed doomed.

However, the fierce energy of the revolutionary government and the sacrifice of thousands of inexperienced soldiers saved the young Republic of France. Not only did the forces under the French flag liberate French territory, but they also invaded foreign soil.

FROM LIBERATION TO CONQUEST

However, old Europe produced a seemingly inexhaustible supply of soldiers to fight against the new republic. Gold from the Bank of England financed coalitions which continually attempted to stifle the spirit of 1789. From 1795 to 1799 the armies of the Republic fought ceaselessly, as the French undertook the conquest of Europe.

The revolutionary leaders destroyed the old order everywhere they went. The peasants were exempted from taxes, tithes, and forced labor. The serfs discovered liberty, and the law became the same for all, as it was in France. In a word, the French armies exported the Revolution.

Though the French were nominally liberating the countries they invaded, they were really most intent on conquest. France, lacking money, pillaged churches and chateaus, drew on the finances of the conquered countries, and imposed a war "contribution" on the inhabitants. This made the French much less popular. The states bordering on the frontiers of the French Republic—Switzerland, Belgium, Holland, and northern Italy—came to be considered annexed and occupied territories. Also, an English blockade of the French coast made commerce in these countries very difficult.

FROM CONSULATE TO EMPIRE

In France, meanwhile, foreign wars took precedence over the internal revolution. Bonaparte, with the help of the 92,000 men of the Imperial Guard, took power on November 9, 1799. He had himself named First Consul, then Consul for life. The consuls of ancient Rome were the highest officials of the city and Napoleon admired ancient Rome's achievements. To follow in the footsteps of Augustus of Rome, Napoleon needed only the title of Emperor. In 1804 he crowned himself emperor, and from that moment nothing seemed to stand in the way of his ambition.

WAR, ALWAYS WAR

From 1804 to 1809 the war did not cease. Napoleon routed the Austrians from Italy and from Germany, and after several attempts, brought the government of Vienna to its knees. The Prussians, who were reputed to have the best army in Europe, were defeated at Jena

The *Grand Empire*

In 1810 the 130 departments of the French Empire covered 750,000 square kilometers. France stretched from the border with Spain to Amsterdam, from Rome to Hamburg.

| FRANCE 30 million inhabitants | ENGLAND 20 million inhabitants | GERMAN STATES 25 million inhabitants | RUSSIA 48 million inhabitants |

in 1806. Russian troops were beaten for the first time with the Austrians at Austerlitz in 1805. After additional victories at Eylau and Friedland in northern Prussia, Napoleon finally imposed an alliance on the czar of Russia, Alexander I.

Now only England remained an invincible enemy. On all the seas, she held the weak French Navy at bay. So the French could no longer maintain ties with what was left of their old colonial empire of the eighteenth century. Bonaparte had already sold Louisiana to the United States. And although some French privateers harassed the English merchants in the Indian Ocean, the English Navy still had the power to attack French Europe at any time or place.

ECONOMIC WEAPONS

To defeat England, Napoleon sought to ruin her economy by preventing her from exporting products to continental Europe. He closed all European ports to English ships and neutral ships carrying English goods. This blockade demanded the permanent presence of the French Army on all borders. Maritime Europe was divided into departments run by French commanders named by the Emperor. They were all under orders to take the most rigorous measures to ensure a Continental blockade. No English merchandise was to be unloaded, not even under a neutral flag. By these measures, Baltic Germany, Holland, and Belgium came under French influence. The country of France, consisting of 130 departments, extended from the left bank of the Rhine and included a part of Switzerland and the western coast of Italy. The Romans were no longer subjects of the pope; a French administrator ruled over them!

THE BONAPARTES REIGNED EVERYWHERE

Napoleon also placed members of his family at the head of a number of "kingdoms." Murat, his brother-in-law, ruled Naples under the name of Joachim I; Jerome, his brother, became king of Westphalia in North Germany; Louis Bonaparte, another brother, had been king of Holland before that country became a French territory in 1810. After the conquest of Spain in 1808, Napoleon put his brother Joseph on the Spanish throne. Naturally, these rulers governed in the exclusive interest of France.

Other territories, which in appearance kept their autonomy, fell more or less under the direct protectorship of the emperor. Napoleon was king of Italy as well as "protector" of the Confederation of the Rhine, which was created from a number of small Germanic states. On the Adriatic coast, he united the Balkan provinces, administered by a governor whom he himself named. He was "mediator" of the Helvetic Confederation, and, finally, the grand duchy of Warsaw fell under his authority.

Prussia's power was minimized, and the czar of Russia was acting as a forced ally. Napoleon had married Marie Louise, the daughter of the emperor of Austria. Thus Napoleon was the absolute master of continental Europe.

FROM DISCONTENT. . .

The inhabitants of all the conquered lands suffered the heavy burden of war to some extent, but the French citizens were the ones who suffered the most. The losses were tremendous: 80,000 men at the Battle of Eylau, 50,000 at Waterloo. In all there were almost a million French victims and probably as many in the allied ranks! At the beginning of the Russian campaign in 1812, Napoleon had 300,000 French soldiers and 350,000 foreign men; after the burning of Moscow, however, barely 20,000 soldiers crossed the Berezina River to return to France.

In the meantime the European economy suffered more and more from the Continental blockade. Activity in the port cities was greatly reduced. The population of Marseilles diminished by one third in fifteen years, and Naples, Barcelona, Bordeaux, and Nantes were on the verge of ruin. The heads of commerce and trade directed their hostility against the regime that threatened to ruin them. Nor did the English fare well. Although they were able to plunder the French colonies, they had to resort to smuggling to get their products into Europe. In addition the long struggle against the French Republic was being financed with English gold.

Inevitably throughout beseiged Europe the winds of resistance began to rise.

Meals in the high schools

Get up	5:30 A.M.
Breakfast	8:00 A.M.
Dinner	12:30 P.M.
Snack	4:45 P.M.
Supper	7:30 P.M.
Bed	8:15 P.M.

Directions for the high schools

—Each school will accept an average of 200 students.
—There will be only six teachers—three for French and Latin studies, three for mathematics.
—Each school will have a penmanship instructor, an art instructor, and a dance instructor.
—After the age of 12, students will take military drill under the direction of a sergeant-major.
—A student who is on detention must stand in the corner of the yard during recess.
—Each school will have a library of 1,500 volumes; the books in these libraries will be identical everywhere.

"Contributions" of war

In 1796 citizens of Milan had already given much gold to France. They then had to furnish as "contributions" of war 2,000 horses; 15,000 uniforms; 100,000 shirts; and 20,000 hats. These demands unleashed violent revolts.

...TO INSURRECTION

In Spain and in Portugal, revolt exploded against the French occupants. The tricolored French flag, symbol of liberation in 1794, now represented oppression. The French fired on rebels in Spain, in Italy, and in the Tyrol. Resistance to French repression took the form of further violence and armed battles.

The French quickly lost their control of Spain and Portugal and their influence in Russia. The reactionary rulers of Vienna and Moscow had no difficulty raising hundreds of thousands of combatants of all nationalities against the Corsican "tyrant." Occupied Europe, wishing to be free whatever the price, no longer recognized French ideas and demanded peace, the peace of the old order.

As oppressive as the French Empire was, however, it had profoundly shaken up the Continent. The liberal ideas of the Revolution penetrated Germany and all of Italy. In Belgium, in Switzerland, and on the left bank of the Rhine, the old laws had been abolished and French laws introduced. The imperial regime was detested because of the burdens it had imposed on the people. It had, however, spread the ideas of justice and equality, ideas which were foreign to the old European monarchies. For this, the rulers of the old order could not forgive Napoleon.

Replacement products

Because of the economic blockades, many plant products from overseas became scarce. To remedy this, replacement plants were sought:
—Woad, cultivated in Alsace, replaced indigo dye.
—Madder-root, cultivated in Provence, replaced cochineal dye.
—An essence extracted from oats replaced vanilla.
—Chicory was added to coffee.
—Linen replaced cotton.
—Beet sugar replaced cane sugar.

The Grand Army

In the summer of 1812 the Grand Army of the French Republic was making its push into Russia. Among the enlisted men were Bavarians, Saxons, northern Germans, Dutch, Italians, Croatians, Poles, and even some Austrians and Prussians who had made an alliance with Napoleon. At the crossing of the Niemen River in western Russia, they were 400,000 strong. They bivouacked for many long hours as they waited to cross over on the three wooden bridges designed by Napoleon. This immense army crossed the river in eight days under the eyes of the Emperor, who watched the maneuver through his field glass.

Hardly had the army arrived in Russia when it had to regroup, since there were many deserters, and many laggards had lost their regiments. The march across Poland had been exhausting. As the troops passed through, the peasants hid their food supplies. Horses died due to the lack of pastureland and watering holes. The officer who commanded the front-line cavalry lost 8,000 horses before reaching Vitebsk!

The weary soldiers carried 30 kilograms of weapons and equipment on their backs. The convoys of livestock did not arrive, for the most part, until the Niemen River was reached. The damp heat of the Russian summer rotted the bread and biscuits in the soldiers' knapsacks and on the few supply wagons. There were no field hospitals to care for the wounded, only makeshift infirmaries along the route.

After a harrowing march the soldiers had to take up their combat positions or start their attack on the run, hungry, sustained only by a mouthful of whiskey. The foot soldiers could never rest, for after an exhausting battle, they either had to pursue the enemy or retreat themselves. On the evening after a victory, when Napoleon presented awards to the survivors, his men had barely enough strength to cry ''Long live the Emperor!'' before collapsing.

Even during bivouac, watch had to be kept.

10

The bridge builders had to work day and night in the rain and under the gunfire of the Austrians to construct this 750-meter bridge across the swift currents of the Danube. But the next day more than a hundred bronze cannons with gun crews, ammunition, spare parts, and supplies crossed over, and the Emperor's army was able to open fire and begin the Battle of Wagram.

The Polish volunteers in the imperial armies kept their national headdress called the chapska. A regiment of their cavalry, which had distinguished itself in Spain, was incorporated into the cavalry of Napoleon's Guard as the famous ''Blue Lancers.''

Barriers had been placed on the mountainous Spanish roads. When the cavalry had cleared a passage, the infantry columns pushed forward. Artillery had to be passed along—sometimes the cannons were unhitched from the horses and pulled up with ropes.

It was the duty of the light cavalry to reconnoiter the army's march and prepare the living quarters. These men are discussing the best farms on which to quarter the officers of the Italian contingent. These troops were to join the Grand Army heading for Russia in 1812.

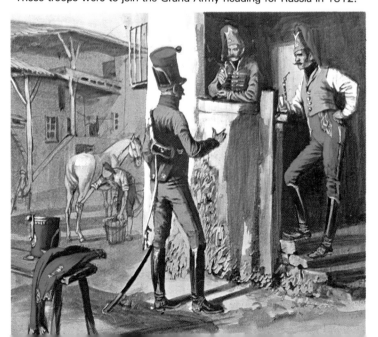

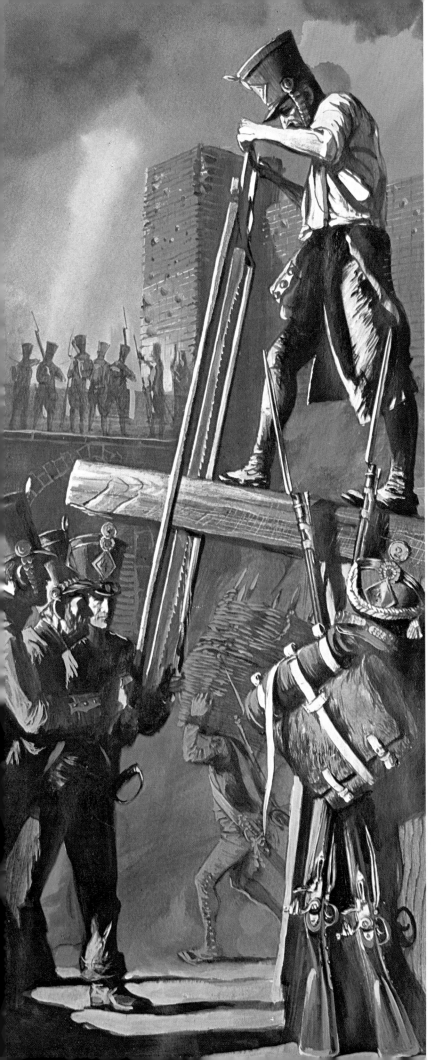

The beginnings of modern warfare

The French Army sometimes waged the old type of siege warfare. This was the kind of warfare used to take Burgos, Spain, in 1808. The French soldiers built high wooden towers from which they hurled cannonballs, brought to a white heat, to start fires. They also brought in heavy cannons which fired only five times an hour. The recoil after each shot was so strong that each time a shot was fired, the cannon had to be repositioned. Because of the stubborn resistance on the part of the Spanish people, these siege tactics were necessary. It was not a regular army that the French faced, but a rebellious population. At Saragossa, it took the French Army three months to seize the city, which they had to take house by house.

More modern military equipment was better adapted to a war on the move, such as Napoleon was waging in other parts of Europe. He had cannons made which fired three shots a minute. In battle he liked to have at his disposition an imposing artillery to break the front ranks of the enemy. At the Battle of Wagram an enormous battery of 100 cannons made a scorching blaze, firing nearly 100,000 cannonballs. At Austerlitz 80 cannons caused the Russians to retreat in complete disarray.

But the manufacture of cannons and guns was a problem. The arsenals could not keep up with the needs of the army. About 145,000 guns were manufactured each year, but 200,000 were needed. At a battle such as the one at Austerlitz, 12,000 muskets were broken or lost. It was necessary to seize the weapons of the enemy. Guns and cartridge cases were taken from the dead and wounded on the battlefield. Toward the end of the Empire, the young recruits were being armed with rifles.

However, on the battlefield, cold-steel combat was still essential. The cavalryman counted on his sword or his lance more than his musket. The infantryman often owed his safety to his bayonet, while the charge of 10,000 horsemen did more for victory than the gunfire of the fusiliers. Although modern in its strategy, Napoleon's army still kept its eighteenth-century armaments.

Constructing siege towers at Burgos in 1808

One minute to load a musket! From left to right: The infantryman of Wurtemberg takes the cartridge from its case. The Hungarian grenadier tears it open. The Scotsman primes (H) the fire pan (C) and closes it with the lock (D). The Italian infantryman puts a bullet and gunpowder into the barrel of the gun and packs it down. When the soldier fires, the impact of the flint (A) against the lock (D) lights the priming powder (F and G). This ignites the charge through a hole in the barrel (B) and opens the fire pan.

The Prussians have just put into firing position a small cannon which can fire three balls a minute with an approximate range of 1,200 meters. The powder and the ball are placed in the muzzle of the cannon, aim is taken, and the linstock lights the powder charge.

When on campaign, the soldiers had to know how to do everything themselves. These light cavalrymen are shoeing their horses. A blacksmith with a forge followed the army, repairing wagons and gun carriages. There were 100,000 horses in the Grand Army.

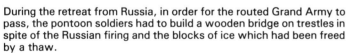

During the retreat from Russia, in order for the routed Grand Army to pass, the pontoon soldiers had to build a wooden bridge on trestles in spite of the Russian firing and the blocks of ice which had been freed by a thaw.

The Englishman Congreve invented a rocket fired by a flintlock. First used in the English navy, then against the French at Leipzig and at Waterloo, it was abandoned because it was essentially inefficient. Only the British "Rocket Corps" used this weapon.

Killing time in temporary quarters

The hard life of a soldier

The soldiers of the Empire were rarely in barracks, since they were almost constantly on campaign. When they were not in battle, they stayed in temporary quarters in cities, in hastily constructed camps in the countryside, or in houses in the villages. Waiting for their orders to fight, they passed time playing cards or dice.

Every day the soldiers went to fencing classes. After the colonel, the master of arms was the most respected person in the regiment. He was the expert in the art of fencing and the ultimate referee in dueling. When a new soldier came into the Grenadier Corps of the Imperial Guard, he was immediately challenged to a duel to prove his valor. If he won, a toast to his health was drunk. Sometimes four cavalrymen from one regiment challenged four from another to defend the honor of their regiments. Although duels were officially forbidden, even the superior officers, who were supposed to enforce this ban, could not resist the challenge and engaged in them.

Food was the greatest concern of the soldiers. Those who were in the Imperial Guard, the Emperor's favorite division, were envied because there were always plenty of provisions ready for them when they entered a town. But most of the time, the troops depended on the peasants for their food, and these soldiers periodically looted the villages. When all reserves were gone, they made flat cakes with grain which they cut in the fields. For meat they ate the flesh of horses that had been killed in battle.

Footwear was the second great worry for the soldier. While the soldiers of the Guard, who always accompanied the Emperor, were transported in wagons, other soldiers had to go on foot. A pair of boots was worn out after 300 kilometers. Ten pairs were needed to go from Paris to Moscow, and each man had only two. French soldiers were seen marching in espadrilles in Spain and in fur boots in Russia. After each battle, it was necessary for the soldiers to find themselves new footwear of some kind.

The village police thrust potential soldiers into the presence of recruiting officers who examined them and measured their height. Then the mayor had each man pick a number from the lottery. Those who drew the unlucky numbers went into military service.

In Poland the peasants hid their provisions from the soldiers in underground caches. But here, Italian soldiers have discovered a hen house and are about to have a feast. Having no regular food supply, the Grand Army had to live by looting.

The Emperor's surgeon was provided with several ambulances for his medical corps. Aid was given to the wounded on the farms surrounding the battlefield. Most wounded arms or legs were amputated at once to avoid gangrene.

Prisoners were often an added burden for an army that was always hungry. These Russians, taken prisoner during the French campaign of 1814, had the good fortune to be fed by villagers who were celebrating Mardi Gras.

In the shops of Moscow, these soldiers found furs, civilian headgear, and women's clothes to protect them from the bitter cold. To keep their faces from freezing, they grimaced constantly. It was far below freezing temperature and the wind was cutting.

Europe's old and new nobility

Time stood still in the courts of central Europe, where people ignored the French Revolution. Napoleon and his decorated field marshals were looked upon as boorish intruders whom the natives were eager to get rid of. These courts were extremely conservative. The great lords of Hungary and Galicia wore the traditional powdered wigs. Francis II, emperor of Austria, did not tolerate the slightest departure from the traditional formalities, in spite of the fact that his daughter Marie Louise married Napoleon in 1810. The courts of Prussia and Russia shared this desire to maintain tradition and to give a sense of discipline and hierarchy to the nobility.

The English, who kept their own royal traditions, plotted behind the scenes to keep Napoleon out of the small courts of Europe, which were not always able to resist the French influence on their own. Most of the German princes submitted to the Rhine Confederation created by Napoleon. But in Italy, the English were more successful—Ferdinand IV, king of Naples, took refuge in Sicily with £400,000 in subsidies sent from London, which were to be used to resist the French. On the other hand Ferdinand III of Tuscany left Florence to accept from Napoleon the grand duchy of Wurzburg in Germany.

Napoleon did not respect the old European nobility. Instead, he brought it under subjection and created his own court of nobles of the Empire. He made his brothers and brothers-in-law kings, each with his own court. Ministers and senators became counts. Mayors and administrators were made barons. Members of the new order of the Legion of Honor became knights. As for the field marshals, they became princes or dukes. Napoleon endowed them generously with substantial incomes and land so that they could live in a manner befitting their titles.

Thus these old soldiers of the wars of the Revolution imitated the royalty of the old prerevolutionary regime, arriving in elaborate carriages at sumptuous balls given in the courtyard of the Tuileries.

The field marshals of the Empire acquired some beautiful land near Paris which had belonged to refugee nobles of the old regime. Imitating the former owners, these revolutionary soldiers hunted with their hounds as the ladies watched from an open carriage.

On ceremonial days in the Empire, as in England, the rulers rode in elaborate carriages decorated with the royal coat of arms. Special workers took excellent care of the elegant harnesses for the eight white horses which drew the state carriage.

Austrian society ridiculed the French military men, who did not know the court customs and danced badly at the balls given at the Imperial Riding School. It was in this society of archduchesses that Napoleon was to find his second wife, Marie Louise.

Napoleon ordered the famous artist David to paint his coronation. The Emperor himself carefully arranged the ceremony and the order of events. He had a model of the ceremony made, with dolls dressed as dignitaries and members of the imperial family. Napoleon demanded that his mother be added to the painting, although she was not at the coronation. Note the decorative bees, Napoleon's symbol.

On the battlefield

This picture shows the battlefield at Waterloo on June 18, 1815. All day long the English forces commanded by the duke of Wellington had withstood charge after charge from the French cavalry by forming themselves into hollow squares with men on all four sides facing out. The squares bristled with the fixed bayonets of the English soldiers which inflicted terrible wounds on the charging enemy soldiers. English cannons, loaded with grapeshot and positioned at the corners of the squares, also caused great damage to the French cavalry. The French artillery was not able to assist the cavalry in its attempts to overcome the English because the heavy gunsmoke decreased visibility and made accurate firing impossible.

Most great battles were won because of the mobility of the victorious armies. In 1800 at Marengo in the north of Italy, Bonaparte took the Austrians by surprise because he was daring enough to march his army across the Alps through the Great Saint Bernard Pass. Napoleon's successful campaign of 1805 was a war of movement in which the brilliant maneuvers of the French Army continually confounded the enemy. However, at Waterloo the Prussian general Blücher, rightly nicknamed General *Vorwärtz*! (Forward!), succeeded in bringing his army by forced marches into Belgium and falling upon Napoleon's right flank in a surprise attack. By their unexpected arrival, the Prussians decided the outcome of the Battle of Waterloo, and the French Army retreated in disarray.

On the battlefield the French infantry attacks were usually made in assault columns. The first ranks, with bayonets attached to their gun barrels, were sacrificed to the enemy fire. Those who followed stepped over the dead bodies of their fallen comrades to gain their position in spite of heavy losses. Grouped behind their flags, the enemy regiments were thus devastated and unable to retreat. If they were attacked by the cavalry and did not have time to form their hollow squares, they broke ranks in utter confusion. In order to win the battle, the infantry had to succeed quickly, without worrying about losses. One out of every two or three soldiers died in battle.

The last stand

The Imperial Guard's light cavalry regiment furnished Napoleon with a permanent escort. This regiment was known for its heroic charges, especially at Austerlitz in 1805 against the czar's horse guard. It also distinguished itself against the Austrian cavalry at Wagram. If Napoleon had used the Guard earlier in the battle of Waterloo, perhaps the outcome would have been different.

The English-Portuguese Army came to the aid of the Spanish, who practiced guerilla warfare against the French. Here they have blown up a bridge, forcing the French soldiers to swim across the river. Guns and powder cases are transported on rafts.

A division of Scottish Highlanders was hurriedly brought from Brussels to Waterloo, under the command of General Picton. Reinforcements such as these came in large numbers to support Wellington's troops and turn the tide against the French Army.

Soldiers often fought to the death to defend their flag. Below, a member of the Royal Scots Greys seizes the flag of the 45th French Regiment. The eagle at the top of the staff is the Napoleonic emblem. The Scots Greys were so called because of the color of their horses.

For the glory of the flag

To the soldier of the French Empire, the flag, or standard, of his regiment was very precious. The presentation of its standard to a regiment was the occasion for solemn ceremony. Napoleon himself had his soldiers swear that they would always defend their standard with their lives. When an attack was made in deep-column formation, the flag was carried up front to lead the troops into battle. Later, when the company regrouped into squares to face the charge of enemy cavalry, the flag was in the center. When their emblem was captured, the ranks tended to break up in confusion.

When flags were captured from the enemy, it was an occasion for great celebration among the troops. The standards taken from the Russians and Austrians during the Battle of Austerlitz were prominently displayed in the parades of the Imperial Guard on its victorious return to Paris.

Napoleon loved pageantry and held many spectacular military ceremonies and parades in Paris. When the French troops entered the city following a victorious campaign, they were always greeted with a spectacular celebration. In 1807 the people of Paris welcomed the troops at the Villette Gate, where a triumphal arch had been constructed. The Imperial Guard opened the parade dressed in full regalia. The grenadiers wore their spats and white trousers. At the head marched the sappers, followed by the drum major and his 24 drummers. Forty-six musicians played the marches of Austerlitz and Marengo, sites of great French victories. After the infantry guard came the grenadier cavalry, mounted on prancing black horses, and then came the white horses carrying 30 trumpeters preceded by the kettle drummer. In the distance, one could see the splendid plumed busbies of the infantry and the bright gold caps of the dragoons.

In 1814, after Napoleon's forces had experienced a number of reversals, 1,417 flags taken from their enemies by the French since 1792 were ceremoniously burned in Paris to prevent their recapture by victorious enemies.

Weapons and flags of Napoleonic Europe

In Amsterdam (above), the alliance between France and Holland was celebrated with joy by the Dutch. But the joy was short-lived. French dominance established, Napoleon enforced a Continental blockade, patrolling ports and coasts. He also conscripted soldiers from among his new allies and taxed the people to pay for his wars. The French quickly became unpopular.

Napoleon made himself king of Italy and his stepson, Eugene Beauharnais, viceroy. In the capital city of Milan, Napoleon sponsored chariot races with the army cavalry. Such extravagant spectacles were very popular among the Italians.

Above are grenadiers of the Imperial Guard. They were recruited from among soldiers who had had at least ten years of brilliant campaigning. They were at least 1.80 meters tall, wore a gold ring in one ear, and sported fierce-looking mustaches.

The cavalry of the Imperial Army consisted of 31 regiments of horsemen who wore green uniforms and curved swords. The elite companies were entitled to wear the busby, a tall fur hat topped by a red pennant. Cavalry parades, preceded by the fanfare of brass bands, were frequent in the cities. Here a crowd is enthusiastically cheering the soldiers.

The ruler of the seas

The English Royal Navy clearly dominated the seas. Its fleet included 115 large warships which carried up to 124 cannons each. It was capable of military landings on any European coast and could block all ports, preventing overseas commerce. From 1805 to 1815 the Royal Navy sank 124 large ships, 157 frigates, and almost 300 smaller boats belonging to its enemies.

As the ruler of the seas of the world, England had to fulfill her missions wherever they might be. When English ships left Portsmouth for the Indian Ocean or the China Sea, they took with them enough fresh water, live sheep, and various other supplies so that they could sail for many months without putting into port. The confined life aboard ship was often difficult for the men, but discipline was maintained at all costs by the ship's officers. At the slightest misdemeanor, the guilty sailor was swiftly punished. He could expect to be put in chains, whipped, or kept on the open deck, with his bare back exposed to the sun.

While English naval power was steadily increasing, France's was in decline. What was left of the once-great French fleet was sent to the bottom of the sea in 1805 during the Battle of Trafalgar in Spain. Many of France's superior naval officers had gone into exile. Because the French fleet was poorly commanded by new, inexperienced officers, Napoleon was unable to achieve his goal of landing his troops in England.

However, France did have privateers based in the Indian Ocean who were very familiar with the coasts of Madagascar and the Comoro Islands, off the coast of Africa. These privateers captured or sank an incredible number of England's rich merchant ships, spreading terror on the route to the Indies. The English chased them in vain, since they could stand up to the best ships of the English Navy. On the sea routes to the Indies or America, London set up convoys of merchant ships escorted by battleships to eliminate the risks of being captured.

Boarding of the *San Nicolas* by Commodore Nelson's ship (Battle of Saint Vincent, 1797)

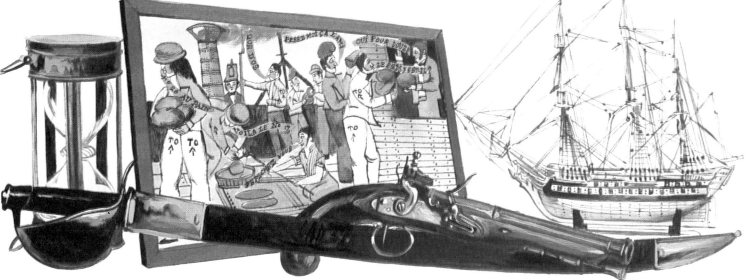

From left to right: A ship's half-hour sandglass, a boarding sword called a ''ladle'' by the crew, a pistol from the English Navy, a drawing by a French prisoner showing the distribution of provisions on an English convict ship, and a model of a warship carefully fashioned in bone or ivory that was made for sale by a prisoner aboard an English convict ship.

Between decks of a ship, under the watchful eyes of a quartermaster, a pump supplies fresh water from a tank in the hold. The men are washing their clothes, which they then put out to dry on the shrouds. But they must not waste a drop. Fresh water is carefully rationed!

In February 1806, a French squadron met the English fleet in the waters off the island of Saint Domingue in the West Indies. Naval battles consisted of two long lines of ships jockeying for position to fire on each other. The heavier vessels had three rows of cannons.

On this frigate, red-hot cannonballs are brought to the gunners, who fire them into the hull of the enemy ship to set it aflame. Nets protect the sailors from pieces of wood shattered by enemy fire. Nets are also spread on the deck for protection against anything that might fall from the rigging during the battle. By the end of a battle, vessels very often had lost their masts.

Citizens and subjects

In all countries dominated by Napoleon, the French tried to establish their own Civil Code, which was supposed to make all citizens equal in the eyes of the law. But for the most part, many European countries still kept their own customs and accepted French law only partially.

In Spain a court that had been in existence since the Middle Ages still met. There were no wigged judges or civil guard—only a group of poor peasants who had been elected by the villagers. The group in the picture below was called the Tribunal on Water and was responsible for judging disputes over irrigation problems. Anyone who was found guilty of attempting to divert his neighbor's share of the water would be heavily fined.

The eastern countries had not yet abolished the practice of slavery. In Russia the serfs had no civil rights or even an identity of their own. They even received their names from their feudal lord, for whom they were forced to work. They had to pay him rents in the form of money or products. In Prussia and Austria the peasants bound to large estates lived under a regime of servitude. Only free men received the benefit of protection under the law.

On the other hand many of the German States, Belgium, and Holland adopted the French Civil Code in 1810. Northern Italy also welcomed the reforms brought by the Civil Code. But the 50,000 priests and 19,000 monks who held the reins of administrative power in the pontifical states ardently resisted the actions of the French prefect in Rome. This official had abolished the Inquisition, taken the Jews out of the ghetto, and established freedom of thought. However, conscription and taxes made the French very unpopular, and in 1815 all the laws which Napoleon had introduced were abolished.

24

A meeting of the Spanish Tribunal on Water

To extend its legislation and apply the Civil Code, the Empire needed jurists. Examinations were given in the 12 law schools, which admitted more than 4,000 students. Under the Empire, 3,600 bachelor's and 76 doctor's degrees in law were granted!

The constabulary did not hesitate to use violence to enforce the law. Here, a village policeman is punishing urchins who have been caught stealing apples. In Paris, people who crossed the street at forbidden places would feel the pointed edge of the guard's bayonet.

At the entrance to all the new police headquarters in Hamburg, Rome, and Antwerp, the coat of arms of Napoleon was hung. This was done to inspire the citizens to take part in the Grand Empire. French was the official language throughout the Empire.

Some convicts in French prisons were forced to work in the ports or in naval arsenals. The scene in the picture below is in Rome, where prisoners are digging in the Palatine Hills and around the Forum, searching for antique monuments.

The Resistance

Dos de Mayo: May 2, 1808. In Madrid French soldiers were being killed in the streets, for the Spaniards did not accept the occupation troops. They did not want to be governed by a French ruler named by Napoleon, and they refused to enforce his Continental blockade against the English.

Reacting immediately, General Murat sent in the soldiers of the Imperial Guard to put down the rebellion and they cut down all who stood in their way. In addition, there were many arrests and house searches. On the next day, May 3, all the suspects who had been arrested were shot without trial. Order reigned in Madrid, but revolt quickly spread throughout other parts of Spain. Thousands of rebels took to the woods and mountains to carry on guerrilla warfare, encouraged by their priests. The Spanish people fed and hid the guerrillas. Napoleon's army arrested and tortured suspects and committed thousands of atrocities in its attempts to discourage resistance.

Many of the peoples who were dominated by the French began to feel strong national sentiment and stood up to the occupying forces. In the peaceful Tyrol in April 1809, Andreas Hofer armed a group of partisans who attacked the French units. In Prussia the old field marshal Blücher secretly reorganized a national army.

Discontent gave rise to active or passive resistance in all the large cities. The inhabitants refused to pay taxes or respond to conscriptions. In the ports, the directives of the French officials, who wanted to prohibit the importation of English merchandise, were ignored. Hamburg, Antwerp, and Rotterdam, ruined by Napoleon's blockade, impatiently awaited their liberation. A Europe of smugglers, defrauders, defaulters, and guerrillas worked patiently but ardently day by day to ruin the Grand Empire.

On May 2, 1808, the French cavalry charges in the streets of Madrid.

In 1801 a black slave named Toussaint L'Overture led a revolt against French rule on the island of Haiti in the West Indies, and proclaimed a constitutional government. Napoleon mounted an expedition against him. Toussaint L'Overture was captured and deported to France. But the blacks, once again slaves, persisted in their revolt, and the devastated French expeditionary corps surrendered.

As Napoleon's army approached, the Russians left Moscow, taking with them all that they could. Soon after they left, most of the city was burned to the ground. The conquering army lost one fourth of its men but found little left to repay the great cost.

At the Brenner Pass, between Italy and Austria, the Tyrolean insurgents attacked the Bavarian troops, who were allies of France. The rebels were commanded by the Tyrolean patriot Andreas Hofer. The rebellion was eventually crushed, and Hofer was executed.

Everywhere in Europe armed rebellion challenged Napoleon's armies, and everywhere members of the resistance were aided by the people. Here two central European guerrillas enter a church to pray while a village woman guards their arms.

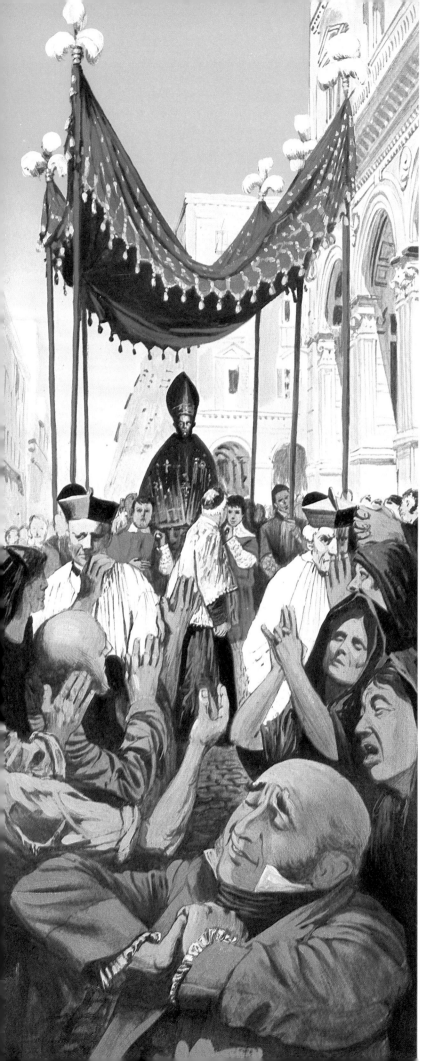

For God and country

After twenty years of war, Europe rediscovered the faith—a mystical, superstitious, and immensely popular faith. In Naples, people were angry with Saint Januarius, who supposedly determined the fate of the French. Every year in Naples, there was a procession honoring this saint. During the ceremony, two vials said to contain the dried blood of the saint were placed against the head of his statue. If the saint favored the celebrants, the blood liquified and came to a boil. This was considered a miracle, and the crowd would react enthusiastically.

In 1799 the Neapolitans did not wish the miracle to take place, because the unpopular French soldiers were among those participating in the procession. But the commander of the French troops whispered something to the clergyman officiating, and the blood liquified. The Neapolitans were very disappointed in Saint Januarius.

This mystical faith was common to all the warring nations, as was the strong dislike for Napoleon, who in 1809 had the pope arrested because the latter would not enforce the Continental blockade in his territory. The Prussian soldiers fought ''for God and country,'' and in German and English caricatures Napoleon was represented as a radical ogre who bullied the Church and detested religion. The war waged by the Spanish was an anti-French crusade led by priests. The czar, head of the Russian Orthodox Church, referred to the French as ''devils,'' and millions of Europeans were convinced that the devil was indeed French.

Many Catholics were indignant at Napoleon's attitude toward the pope. The Church in France, which at the beginning supported the Empire, became dissident. Young priests again took on political missionary activities in a country de-Christianized by the Revolution. The intellectuals were sympathetic to this revival, and many people with complaints against the French regime found their way back to the Church.

A procession in honor of Saint Januarius in Naples

28

The Spanish Church, whose members believed that all power came from God, rejected French ideas. The priests and monks urged on the religious Spanish people and trained them for resistance against the French. Guerrilla warfare became a holy war against the French.

In 1801 the papacy reluctantly signed a concordat with Napoleon. The Empire became responsible for the maintenance of the churches and for paying the clergy. The pope consecrated the bishops, but Napoleon appointed them, and they had to swear allegiance to him.

Greece and Russia remained faithful to Orthodox Christianity. Here a priest is baptizing a child in a Russian village. The priests taught the peasants to love God, the czar, and their lords. The czar himself was venerated as a representative of God.

The Protestants of Germany were not at all bothered by the French occupation. Napoleon's Civil Code stressed the equality of religions, and this Protestant marriage could not have taken place in Catholic Austria, where Protestants did not have the rights of citizenship.

Jews of Alsace are reading from the Torah, which is written entirely by hand. They wear the traditional prayer shawl and skullcap. The Revolution gave full civil rights to the Jews. They had their own synagogue, which could hold 2,000 congregants.

The Continental blockade

The English organized convoys of merchant ships which sailed under the protection of the Royal Navy in order to assure the continuation of commercial traffic with America. But sometimes a vessel, turned off course and damaged by a storm, would be forced to heave to and await help. The damaged English brig in the picture below has been sighted and attacked by a French privateer.

Incidents of this kind were very common on the high seas. The French Navy, badly beaten at the Battle of Trafalgar, had not been rebuilt. It was mainly the privateers who troubled the English convoys. And Napoleon, by decreeing a blockade against England, also considerably hampered her trade with Europe; every English ship that entered a blockaded European port was considered lawfully captured. Neutral ships that transported English merchandise were in danger of being seized and their cargoes destroyed. No ship could approach the European coast if it had stopped at an English port.

These measures only served to encourage smug-

gling. In 1811, French officials discovered 417 bolts of cloth being secretly imported into France in a cannonship! Although smugglers were threatened with a branding from red-hot irons, they still had constant dealings with such Rhine cities as Strasbourg and Mainz. However, the smugglers sometimes suffered losses, as when troops surrounded Frankfurt, the center of the contraband traffic, and seized enormous quantities of merchandise.

France's own ports came very close to ruin. The merchants of Bordeaux, Nantes, and Marseilles could not resort to smuggling as those in other European cities like Genoa, Hamburg, or Bremen were able to. In 1789 there were 320 ocean-going ships that left Marseilles. In 1811 there were only 9, and the population of the city had dropped from 120,000 to 90,000. The disappearance of commerce caused a decline in industry. Obsessed by his struggle against England, Napoleon turned a deaf ear to all reason.

An English brig is attacked by a French privateer. To hamper the assailants, nets have been placed around the deck.

In Antwerp, English merchandise has been seized. It had been secretly unloaded from a Swedish ship flying a neutral flag. The blockade had to be rigorously enforced to ruin English commerce and industry. Cloth from London, tea from India, and sugar from the West Indies were burned or thrown into the sea. The naval commander-in-chief of the Empire personally supervised the operation above.

There was strict control of merchandise on the roads and at the entrances to the cities. This German merchant must show his declaration papers, which permit him to move around, at an urban military post commanded by a French soldier.

The Bavarians resorted to all sorts of subterfuge to surreptitiously bring forbidden merchandise into their cities. The guard is not searching this hearse, which happens to be loaded with coffee beans! Coffee and tobacco were highly valued.

The English dropped off their merchandise on small islands near the large ports. The smugglers then picked it up in the darkness of night. The islands around Naples were infested with contrabandists. The island of Helgoland, near Hamburg, was one of the large drop-off points. English merchandise thus found its way into the ports of Bremen and Hamburg right under the noses of the French soldiers!

Policing the Empire

When Napoleon came to power, he seemed to be destined to restore order out of the chaos brought on by the French Revolution. He had two enemies—on the left were the Jacobins, radicals who were still dedicated to the ideas of the Revolution; on the right were the Royalists, who were dedicated to the restoration of the monarchy. Because he wanted to become emperor and suppress the liberties of the Republic, Napoleon struck down the Jacobins, although they did not plot against him. He also put down the Royalist movement, which was the only one that actually organized plots against him.

Napoleon's police organization was quite impressive. The national armed police force, under the ministry of war, was organized in 1801. The minister of police, Fouché, relied on a network of undercover agents, whom he sometimes chose from among former convicts, to carry out the pursuit of suspects. He kept an eye on the journalists; created a press bureau that censored newspapers; and periodically inspected theaters, printers, and bookstores.

The country was divided into four large police districts. These districts were directed by councillors of the state who had been named by Napoleon and were under the authority of the minister of police. These councillors were kept informed by general commissioners, of whom there were about thirty in all of France, and by police commissioners from the cities.

The department of foreign affairs had its own police force, which kept it informed of the activities of foreigners and of their agents in France. The ministry of finance policed the postal service, and its ''black cabinet'' did not hesitate to open mail. The ministry of the interior and the ministry of war also had their own police agents. There was nothing that could escape the watchful eye of Napoleon.

All attempts at conspiracy against the Empire were systematically foiled. The conspirators were shot and their accomplices were thrown into prison. The opponents of Napoleonic politics, literature, and art were exiled. The Empire was a veritable police dictatorship.

An undercover agent, one of Fouché's spies

There were many conscripts who, having drawn an unlucky number, refused to go to the barracks—they deserted. In the north, center, west, and southwest of France, the deserters formed bands of outlaws, pursued by the military police but protected by the people.

Along with the Jacobins, the Royalists strongly resisted. Seized in a small neutral town east of the Rhine, the duke of Enghien, an important Royalist, was accused of treason, hastily judged by a military tribunal, and executed on March 21, 1804.

Beginning in 1801 special French tribunals judged political opponents without jury and without appeal. The police were authorized to search the homes of suspects, and no one was safe from house search.

Napoleon Bonaparte's life was in danger on several occasions, but each attempt on his life served as a pretext to arrest opponents. In 1800 an attempt in the Rue Saint-Nicaise, although perpetrated by the Royalists, allowed the police to arrest 130 Jacobins.

Bonaparte took from the municipalities the right to name their own police commissioners. From March 8, 1800, he became the chief of police and assigned the prefects. The ministry of the interior and the ministry of police worked together in their hunt for dissidents.

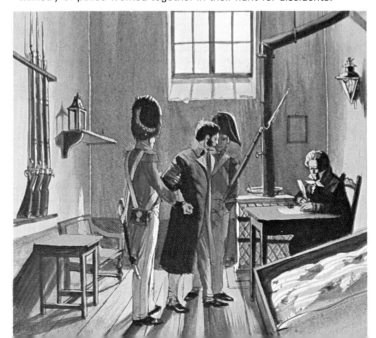

French soldiers in Egypt

A blending of cultures

Since the early days of the French Revolution, and even before, numbers of French left their homeland to live in exile, bringing much of their culture and skills with them. As early as 1789, members of the French aristocracy and clergy fled the country and settled in other countries, particularly in the Rhineland, the Netherlands, and England.

Many French fled the Revolution and, a little later, deserted Napoleon and took refuge in Russia. Most of these emigrants never returned to France, and Russia was greatly influenced by French culture, including manners, styles, food, and even the French language. About 25,000 Royalists crossed the border of the Grand Empire, many of them finding a welcome in the court of the czar. The philosopher Joseph de Maistre settled in St. Petersburg, while Duke Richelieu became a tutor to the czar at Odessa. Madame de Staël, a French author renowned for her wit and brilliance, was pursued by Napoleon's police. She escaped to Switzerland, traveled to Sweden, and went on to England. Many emigrants found their way to London, including the future king Louis XVIII in 1807.

One of the most noted French emigrants was the author and philosopher Viscount François René de Chateaubriand. Disillusioned with the French Revolution, he left for the United States in 1791. He recorded his many adventures, real and imaginary, in his famous *Voyage en Amerique*. He returned to France, only to flee from Napoleon's excesses. He traveled in Greece, Egypt, Palestine, and Turkey, spreading his own brand of French thought.

Ordinary Frenchmen also helped to blend French culture with that of other countries. For twenty years, thousands of French soldiers waged wars in most parts of the Continent. Many of the soldiers in these Napoleonic wars were taken prisoner. But at that time there were no prison camps. Only the English and the Spanish of Cadiz kept their prisoners chained on convict ships. Neither the Russians nor the Prussians paid much attention to prisoners of war. Many Frenchmen, instead of trying to escape, settled in the lands of their captors.

During the French Revolution, tens of thousands of emigrants settled in Germany at Koblenz and in England, Russia, Prussia, and Italy. In England, many refugees who did not return to France after 1800 earned a living by giving French lessons.

French prisoners in Russia did not live in camps. If they were not massacred by the Cossacks, they found work on the farms and became integrated with the Russian people. Here these former soldiers are employed in a sawmill in a large Russian forest.

Never had such a migration of armies swept through Europe. They came from the English Channel to the Volga. Hundreds of thousands of European fighters sometimes had the opportunity to fraternize. At Tilsit, Russian and French grenadiers join together in a banquet.

In 1814, the Prussian Guard set up its bivouac in the Luxembourg Gardens in Paris. These "hussars of death," like the English and the Russians, gave concerts in the public squares. They paraded on the Champs Élysées, where the Cossacks were encamped.

For 20 years, the French occupied the left bank of the Rhine. These soldiers, parading in the streets of Frankfurt, at first were not considered enemies. In this region of Germany, national sentiment awakened slowly.

Wartime farming

In 1811 embattled Europe experienced a serious agricultural crisis. As harvests everywhere were poor, the price of wheat increased. Bread, which usually cost 2 sous a pound, was selling in France for 12 sous. The richer farmers stockpiled their grains in hopes that they could sell them later at a higher price. This caused the government to send police into the countryside to set price ceilings and to insist that the farmers declare their inventories. However, luckily for the farmers, the crisis lasted only a year and by 1812 the grain harvests were once again excellent.

Wine was plentiful in Europe and was exported everywhere except to England, because of the blockade. The raising of horses and cattle increased. Sheep raising for the textile industry, also increased, but only England had cotton to weave. Two plants which had recently been introduced to Europe were becoming the universal foods of the poor. These plants were potatoes, which became indispensable during the crisis of 1811, and tomatoes.

The Continental blockade forced growers to make enormous efforts to find other products to replace those which had become unavailable. The Belgians roasted the roots of chicory to replace coffee, which only the English could still obtain. The French of the southwest planted tobacco, and the Germans and Flemish developed the cultivation of the sugar beet. Over 200,000 acres of crops were planted in France.

In England, agriculture had already become carefully regulated and scientific. Farmers there used fertilizer and practiced crop rotation. But the farmers on the Continent still adhered to the traditional technique of letting the land rest one out of every two or three years. Even though they had been liberated from the feudal regime, the peasants of western Europe still had to submit to government rules concerning use of the land. The town assembly regulated cultivation. The citizens had to struggle to hold on to whatever property they had acquired and to prevent the government's sheep from grazing on their lands.

The police and army requisitioning grain in 1811

Burgundy wine was very popular in Europe, and the owners of the famous vineyards became very rich. Wine was exported as far as Moscow. Giant presses such as the one above made it possible to process large quantities of grapes.

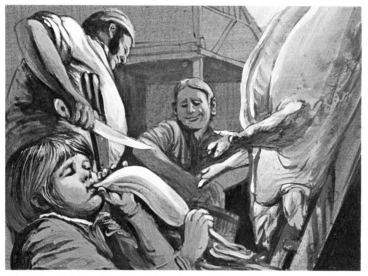

It is festival time in a Bavarian village! A pig has been killed, and a little boy is blowing up its bladder to make a balloon. According to tradition, the women collected the blood to make sausage and for several days the people danced and celebrated.

Bullfighting had already been practiced in Spain for more than a hundred years. The bulls were raised on the great plains of Andalusia without ever seeing a man. Here, Portuguese riders are choosing animals for the fight by testing their combativeness.

This Swiss farmer warms the curdled milk from his cows in a large copper cauldron to make cheese. When the milk becomes clotted, he will draw the caked cheese up from the bottom of the pot with a piece of cloth.

On the vast Hungarian plains, the young people who were not in the cavalry raised horses or became shepherds. They built reed huts for protection from the weather, and their drinking water came from wells that they had dug in the plains.

Industry and finance

To manufacture thousands of bronze cannons and hundreds of thousands of iron guns, more and more foundries were needed. At the battle of Leipzig in 1813, soldiers in the French Army used more than 400,000 bullets! The armaments industry developed considerably everywhere because of the wars. The shipbuilding industry also prospered, particularly in England.

Iron was still melted in forges by heat from charcoal. But in England and parts of Germany and France, coal-burning blast furnaces were already being used. There were 200 blast furnaces in France, producing 112,000 tons of iron. Throughout Europe the technology of metallurgy progressed.

The manufacture of textiles was one of the best-developed industries throughout many parts of Europe. England spun and wove cotton that was imported from America and wool from its own sheep, as well as flax and hemp. In France there were also large wool-weaving factories particularly in the city of Reims and throughout the Normandy region. Because of a short-age of raw materials, there was no cotton being woven in France, but the silk industry prospered there and in some villages in northern Italy. More than 15,000 workers were employed in the silk factories of Lyons.

War and industry both required financing. The large English banks dominated Europe because of their ability to extend credit and finance the coalitions against Napoleon. Amsterdam lost its importance as a financial center. Napoleon himself created the Bank of France, which regulated the price of silver. Speculators were able to make fortunes by lending money at high interest rates to industrialists who were working to produce supplies for the army. But the absence of important international commerce and the difficulty of overland communication severely hampered the development of capitalism. Even England, the ruler of the seas, suffered a slump in credit and production. Without peace and security, investment in industry was a poor risk.

Prosperous armaments factories still used eighteenth-century techniques.

All sorts of indigents arrived in Paris each morning to ask for financial aid from the rich financiers. These moneylenders and army contractors distributed alms to those who came begging for them—a poet without an editor, a sculptor without a commission, a would-be inventor, a mother whose husband has deserted the family, a loser in the national lottery.

At Lloyd's of London, the famous naval insurance company, armaments manufacturers and ships' captains attempted to collect insurance money for their lost cargoes. But the seizures by French privateers were very difficult to prove.

There was a lack of indigo, a blue dye from overseas, because of the blockade. So an herb called woad was grown in Alsace and the southwest part of France to dye uniforms blue. Here strands of wool are being dipped into the dye and then dried in hanks.

Workers had to have a ledger in which they recorded their dates of employment and discharge, their absences, and above all any salary advances. Since they could not get work elsewhere if they did not present a ledger, they were kept under the thumb of their employer.

The English loved two wines—Bordeaux and port. Since they could not obtain the Bordeaux because of Napoleon's blockade, they drank a good deal of port as soon as Portugal was liberated by Wellington. The English buyers were careful to taste before they bought.

The Empire sets a new style

The furniture makers of the French Empire were outstanding craftsmen. The designs they executed were characterized by simple, symmetrical, rather formal lines and somewhat heavy proportions. The styles reflected Napoleon's preference for the grandeur of classical antiquity, particularly that of imperial Rome. Gone were the intricately carved and gilded pieces of Louis XIV. Gone, too, were the gracefully simple, light, and dainty styles of Louis XVI. Instead, a more constrained, dignified, heavily impressive mood prevailed.

Parisian cabinetmakers used valuable woods, such as ebony, citrus, and maple. But their preference was mahogany, finely crafted, with little gilding or carving but ornamented with beautifully modeled bronze or brass decorations.

As the popularity of the new designs spread throughout Europe, other Parisian craftworkers were also in great demand. Bronze objects, printed silks, rich velvets, wool rugs, fine porcelain and glass, and elegant tapestries, all created in the new Empire style, were much sought after by members of fashionable society.

While styles in women's clothes changed rapidly, the typical Empire style dresses also showed the influence of what French designers believed to be classical antiquity. The gowns were simple, usually made of lightweight cotton, with low necklines and very high waistlines. The graceful dresses fell to the ground in soft, straight folds.

The elaborate wigs of earlier decades were no longer worn by the ladies of the French Empire. Instead, a woman wore her own hair rather short, reflecting a classical influence, in this case from ancient Greece. Fashionable hairdressers made a great deal of money catering to the tastes of society ladies. Napoleon's Paris was even more costly than that of Louis XVI.

40

These chairs and their decorations were inspired by antiquity.

Not far from Versailles in a town called Jouy-en-Josas, craftsmen made printed linen cloth. The printed and dried cloth was plunged into running water and then laid on a fulling board to thicken the cloth and set the colors. After being soaked again for 24 hours in running water, the cloth was stretched on the ground and sprinkled to prevent it from drying too quickly, which would fade the colors. For the final process, the linen was dipped into a boiling solution of cow dung. Cloth from Jouy was in great demand.

Wrought-iron gates required very detailed adjusting before they were hung. The new rulers of imperial Europe had chateaus built for themselves with grillwork equal in beauty to that at Versailles. Nothing was too good for them!

In Paris, cloth was measured by the meter. The metric system, adopted by the revolutionary government, was used in all the shops. It soon spread throughout Europe except England, where measurements continued to be made in feet and inches.

The people of the large European capitals were enthusiastic walkers. They walked for miles in dirty and often muddy streets, so wearing boots was a necessity. To save wear and tear, English shoemakers had the excellent idea of putting horseshoes on the heels.

The Swiss, the southern Germans, and the French from the Jura Mountains were renowned for their skill in the manufacture of watches and clocks. These skilled craftsmen would travel around the countryside to repair the products of the local craftsmen.

New highways for Napoleonic Europe

England controlled the seas. If Napoleonic Europe wished to survive, it would have to develop efficient means of transportation and communication across the Continent. Napoleon may not have been convinced of the future of the new railroads, but he was well aware of the necessity for a good network of transportation routes, for the sake of commerce and industry as well as for military purposes.

Waterways were given first priority. Canalboats and barges could carry the heaviest cargoes, such as metal ores and coal. So riverbeds were deepened and France's already fine system of canals was extended. The Rhine, Rhône, Somme, and Schelde rivers were connected by canals. Important canals connected Paris with Lyons and Marseilles with Amsterdam in Holland. The joining of the Rhine with the Meuse by canal made possible the manufacture of iron in the Lorraine region of France and connected this area with the greatest water routes in Europe. But it took a month for canalboats to go from Arles to Lyons, a distance of about 250 kilometers.

For faster transportation, highways were used. Napoleon's engineers repaired or constructed thousands of miles of road all over Europe. These included those over the Simplon and Mont Cenis passes in the Alps. In 1810 about 3,000 passenger carriages and 14,000 cargo wagons used the Mont Cenis Road, which connected Italy with Lyons. Along the Mediterranean coast Napoleon had the famous mountainous Corniche Road rebuilt from Nice, France to Genoa, Italy. And over 200 major highways went from Paris to various parts of Europe.

But there were many pitfalls which came between the plans of the engineers and the realization of their projects. Napoleon himself experienced the inconvenience of one of these in 1815 on his escape from Elba. When he wanted to use the road that went from Cannes to Grenoble, he had to walk 100 kilometers on a mule path because the road was not completed!

A difficult passage on the Simplon road at the exit of a long tunnel

Canalboats were a much more comfortable means of travel than were stagecoaches. In countries such as Holland where waterways abounded, travelers gladly chose this method of travel. Regular service linked the principal cities. The boats on the canals were drawn by horses that walked along the banks. Heavy goods were also transported on these waterways.

On all the government roads at the entrance of a province or city, travelers had to pay a special tax levied on each person and on all goods. The tollhouses which were set up at all the gates of Paris in the eighteenth century greatly hampered traffic.

In England the mail carriages went much faster than the heavy stagecoaches, but there were very few seats. The post drivers wore special reinforced boots to protect them against the shock of the car-

The stagecoaches traveled 75 kilometers in 24 hours, frequently stopping to change horses. It took six days to go from Lyons to Paris. When evening came, the stagecoach travelers stopped at a roadside inn to dine and spend the night.

riage poles when the horses ran at a trot. The boots also protected them from fractures in case of a fall. There were frequent accidents because of broken axles.

Advances in science and technology

In England the railroad age was in its infancy. Richard Trevithick built the first steam engine that could pull passenger cars along tracks. It was called the *Catch Me Who Can* and ran around a circular track. For a few shillings in London in 1808, people could ride in this newfangled contraption, which was thought of as little more than a fairground attraction.

In France there was even less general interest in railroads, although experiments using steam power in transportation were made there as early as 1802. Steam was also used as energy in the textile mills and for hauling coal in the mines. When Robert Fulton's steamboat was first demonstrated in France in 1803, it did not find many strong supporters.

Napoleon's interest in science and technology was primarily in the hope that they could be made to serve French industry. He visited factories and encouraged inventors and scientists. Most of the improvements in technology in France were made in the textile industry.

The art of jacquard weaving revolutionized the silk industry. Joseph-Marie Jacquard introduced his new weaving machine in 1801, and by 1810 the silk mills in Lyons were turning out the mechanically woven fabric with its complicated patterns on almost 11,000 looms. French chemists also made it possible to weave linen that was superior to cotton.

The first soda-ash works was started at Chauny in 1806. Production of chlorine, sulfuric acid, and bleaches was widely expanded, and the use of potassium chloride as fertilizer became more widespread. With the work of Berthelot, Gay-Lussac, and Thénard, chemistry took giant steps forward. Volta in Italy and Davy in England laid the foundations of electrochemistry, and in London, Murdock and Clegg produced gas for lighting.

Trevithick's first train

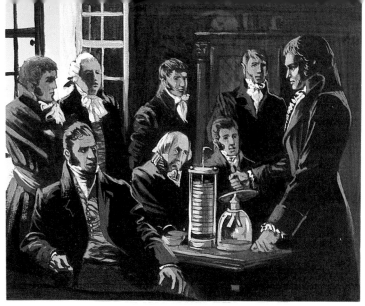

Alessandro Volta, a famous Italian physicist, performs a demonstration for his French colleagues of the Academy of Sciences. The thin gold sheets of an electroscope separate, showing the passage of an electric current.

On August 9, 1803, Robert Fulton, the American inventor, demonstrated his steamboat on the Seine in France. Napoleon was interested in this invention, but the Institut National de France rejected it after several experiments. (The picture shows Fulton's *Clermont* in 1814.)

The whitish syrup extracted from the sugar beet was poured into molds, where it hardened into loaf-shaped blocks of sugar. The extraction of sugar from the sugar beet was a Prussian invention which was developed and used during the Continental blockade.

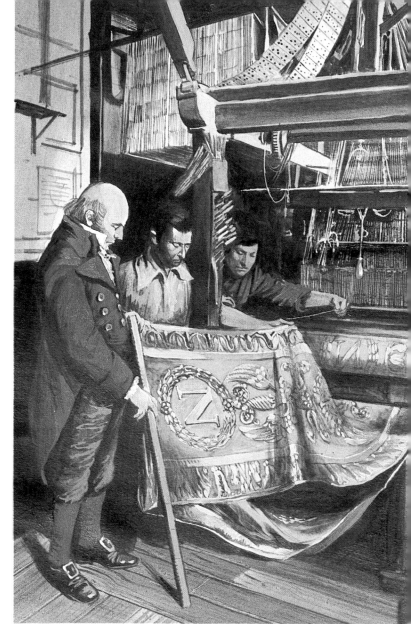

On this jacquard loom a steel comb controlled the threads; the comb had a tooth for each of the 4,000 threads. The silk weaver could usually weave three or four meters of silk in a 12-hour day, but only three or four centimeters of the design was complicated.

Workers are building a tower for a "visual telegraph." Invented by the Chappé brothers, this instrument used movable arms to transmit words to the next tower within sight. Such stations, set 15 or 16 kilometers apart, could rapidly transmit messages across France.

Children teach illiterate soldiers to read. It is their only hope for promotion.

Schools and universities

Seventeen years of army service! The Emperor himself wanted to promote him to second lieutenant right on the battlefield. But his captain objected—the old sergeant did not know how to read! There were a great many incidents like this in Europe. Raised in the country, these men had never gone to school. In the picture above, schoolchildren are shown teaching some old French soldiers to read—an interesting solution to the problem.

There were almost no primary schools in most of central and eastern Europe. The village clergymen taught the fundamentals to a few children. In Germany and in England, however, the school systems were more developed. Children from wealthier families paid for their schooling, but instruction was free for poorer students.

In France, Napoleon was not very concerned about primary schools, but he did create 45 high schools, and four of these were in Paris. Such schools assured the sons of middle-class French citizens a solid

secondary-school education. The students in these schools were required to wear uniforms, and the teachers wore tricornered hats and long black robes with white ties. As well as learning the usual academic subjects, students were also taught how to handle weapons. Unruly students were subject to severe punishment; if they misbehaved enough they might even be arrested and thrown into prison.

A small minority of youths in some of the countries of western Europe went to colleges and universities. The German universities were the most famous, and students from all over Europe came to study there. In France, one of the best-known universities was the École Polytechnique. Here engineers and technicians studied the physical sciences and their application to warfare. The great Institut National de France taught the sciences, French language and literature, history, and art. However, law schools were the most popular. It almost seemed that there was greater need for civil servants, judges, and lawyers than for engineers.

In the art schools of Italy, students devoted themselves to the concentrated study of anatomy. Plaster models enabled them to copy with great precision all the details of the human body.

In this school in Bavaria, a student is being punished. If he moves, the bells on his cap will ring, and he will be beaten. Another boy kneels on the edge of a log to learn the alphabet.

The students at the École Polytechnique benefited from the latest scientific progress. The work of physicists Coulomb of France and Volta of Italy produced the first storage batteries, giving pupils the opportunity to study the effects of electrochemistry.

Fencing was practiced among the upper classes throughout Europe. At an early age, children had to learn to defend themselves and to ride a horse. Swords were still the basis of all military exercises, and fencing teachers were generally former soldiers.

Popular sports

In the Tuileries Gardens in Paris, a strange machine appeared for the first time in 1791. It was to become the ancestor of the modern bicycle. It had no chain or gears; there was only a simple wooden bar placed on top of two wheels. The bar often had a horse's head on one end and a tail at the other! The rider sat on a hard seat and grasped the handlebars. Riding this contraption became a popular sport, although there were no bicycle races such as those that are enjoyed in France today.

There were horse races, however, and fashionable people enjoyed watching the stallions run at a racetrack near Paris. The beautiful horses were perfectly groomed and their harnesses were dazzling. Horse races were also a traditional favorite in Italy. But the paradise of horse racing was England where it was extremely popular. People in England could also watch rowing races on the River Thames. Boxing matches, too, were popular among the gentlemen. In Spain, bullfights became increasingly popular.

There were practically no sports in which students might participate in European schools except in Germany and at some English colleges. In France, former soldiers taught students fencing with foils, swords, sabers, and cudgels. Swimming instructors were rare. However, in Paris, one might occasionally see young people diving off barges and swimming nude in the Seine.

Rural Europe still depended a great deal on the horse. All country children were good horseback riders. In fact, nearly every young peasant became a rider skilled enough to be able to serve in the cavalry. Young people of the upper-class in England rode magnificent horses and took part in fox hunts. Deer hunting became popular in France, and the abolition of feudal privileges in western Europe made it possible for peasants to openly hunt rabbits with dogs and guns. Hunting and fishing were by far the most popular sports in Europe.

Cycling in the Tuileries Gardens during the Revolution

The Swiss learned wrestling techniques while serving in Europe's armies. These former soldiers are giving an exhibition not far from the old town of Basle. The spectators cheered the wrestlers and made bets. There were wrestling matches at all the big fairs.

This powerful Turk is swimming across the Bosporus Strait. The French naval officers imprisoned on ships at Cadiz were unable to escape because they did not know how to swim. Swimming was not a very popular sport at the time.

The Flemish enjoyed the sport of archery, which had a tradition that went back to the Middle Ages. The medals worn by this archer were awarded to him during earlier meets. At the entrance to the archery range, a sign in Flemish reads, ''Swearing is forbidden.''

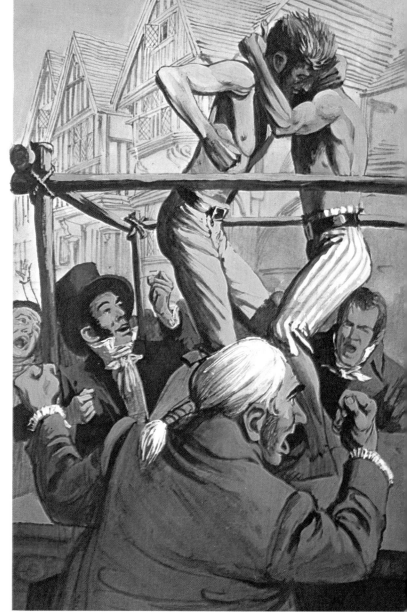

Boxing rings were set up in some towns so that people could attend boxing matches. This violent sport was imported from England, where it was very popular. At the time, boxing had very few fixed rules. Military men did not indulge in the sport.

Diabolo, a popular game of the time, came from Italy. The object was to make the top jump on the cord by briskly maneuvering the two sticks. Children were not the only ones who played diabolo. So did the pretty young women!

Public entertainments

In Europe's capitals on Sundays, crowds strolled endlessly along the boulevards. The great avenues of Vienna, Berlin, and St. Petersburg were filled with elegant horses pulling the gilded carriages of fashionable ladies and gentlemen. London, Rome, and Paris had beautiful large parks. In Paris the Tuileries Gardens, the Luxembourg Gardens, the Botanical Gardens, and the gardens of the Palais-Royal were always filled with people. Around the Palais-Royal, one could find all kinds of entertainment—billiard games, silhouette cutters, cafés, bookstalls, and many restaurants and small shops.

The big cities had all kinds of diversions. At Vauxhall in London and at Tivoli in Paris, there were street performers as well as public ballrooms where people enjoyed a daring new dance imported from Germany—the waltz! At Tivoli, hot-air balloonists gave demonstrations and released the first parachutes. People could also attend a performance of the Franconi Brothers Circus, famous for its horseback riders. But many people enjoyed simply strolling around the Turkish Gardens and enjoying the sights. They might watch the "human top," a 12-year-old girl who could spin like a top for 30 minutes at a time. They might see a two-headed calf, a sheep with five feet, or miniature carriages harnessed to fleas. They might watch flies fighting duels with pins or gaze at a young woman who sported a meter-long beard! One might even have the opportunity to have one's fortune told by a dog using playing cards!

In England, cockfights were all the rage in working-class neighborhoods, while in Spain, carnivals filled the streets with joyous and unruly crowds of people, freed for a few days from the constraints of poverty.

50

At the entrance to the Turkish Gardens, children ride in a carriage pulled by a Saint Bernard.

Puppet theaters were popular throughout Europe. Puppets were slipped on over the hand like a glove. But marionettes were jointed figures that worked by attached strings. The Italians, especially the Sicilians, were famous for their marionettes.

At carnival time the poorest, most oppressed people could take a kind of revenge on society. The famous artist Goya painted a tragic carnival where the starving people, in devil costume, found enough strength to play the castanets and defy society.

Country fairs were a tradition in the Netherlands. The whole village took a holiday. Beer and wine flowed freely. Italian actors on raised platforms presented pantomimes and there were contests and races. At night young and old gathered around the musicians to dance.

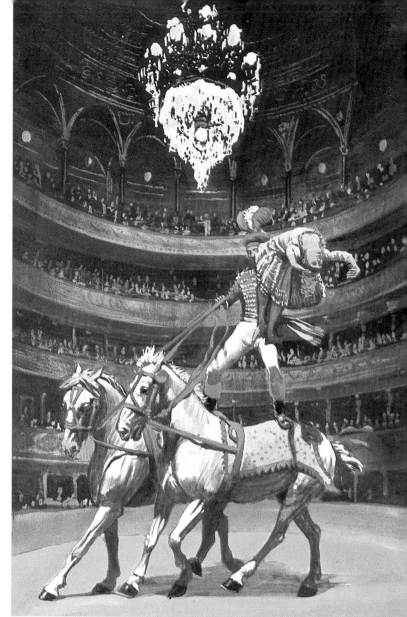

The great Franconi Brothers Circus had been popular in Paris since 1807. This famous group presented pantomimes on horseback in a resplendent setting. In the mornings the Franconi brothers gave riding lessons to young noblemen.

The Café Frascati was a meeting place for elegant Parisians. There was room for 2,000 people to dance, and suppers were served in the gambling rooms. When the famous hostess Juliette Récamier visited there, she was nearly suffocated by an admiring crowd.

French workers in Rome build a section of the city in the classical style.

Architects and city planners

Under the direction of the well-known architect Guiseppe Valadier, the French constructed an entire section of Rome around the Piazza del Popolo. Valadier was inspired by the work of the Parisian architects Charles Percier and Pierre Fontaine. The neoclassic style of architecture was popular at the time. This style was characterized by colonnades, richly decorated pediments, and massive stairways decorated with statues and monuments.

Napoleon's dream was to restore the capitals of Europe in the neoclassic style. But in Berlin and Vienna, the style of the past century still prevailed. While in London, architects were being inspired by the Gothic style of the medieval cathedrals. The most important realizations of Napoleon's dream were in Paris. City planners designed a triumphal route from the old Place de l'Étoile to the Bastille. The route went through the gardens of the Louvre and down the Rue de Rivoli. In 1806, Chalgrin began work on the Arc de Triomphe. Percier and Fontaine were building the

smaller Arc du Carrousel and arcaded mansions along the new Rue de Rivoli. They also planned the Tuileries Gardens. Brongniart constructed the Bourse (the stock exchange) and designed the famous Père-Lachaise Cemetery. Around the Place de l'Étoile wide avenues were also laid out. The city of Paris began to grow and expand toward the west.

But in Paris, as in London and in Vienna, most streets were narrow, dirty, winding, and dark. In Paris, 4,000 streetlights cast a pale light and blew out at the least breeze. Europe's capitals, in general, were unsafe at night.

Water was scarce and expensive. Garbage was dumped into the rivers, and the cities' water supplies were often polluted, causing serious epidemics of dysentery in the summer. Houses, heated only with wood-burning fireplaces and lit with candles, were cold and uncomfortable. Even Napoleon, while working at night, tied a kerchief around his head to protect himself from drafts.

London was the first city in Europe to have gaslights. William Murdock and Samuel Clegg developed the system. The gas was produced by coal, which was plentiful in England, rather than by charcoal, which was used in France.

Spectators shivered as they left this splendid theater in St. Petersburg, where winter temperatures reached −30°C. Their drivers drank vodka and warmed themselves at an open fire to keep from freezing while waiting for their masters.

Rome was still the papal city. Thousands of clergymen visited Rome, but ordinary tourists were rare. Only artists like David or writer-philosophers like Chateaubriand were interested in the ruins that today attract people from all over the world. Laundresses hung their

Plans were made to build a bronze elephant on the Place de la Bastille in Paris. It was to be cast in metal from captured Spanish cannons. The statue was to be huge and fitted with a decorative fountain. However, only a wood-and-plaster model was actually built.

wash to dry in the Forum, and armies of cats made their home among the ancient stones. Important papal administrators lived in splendid palaces, but there was little industrial activity, and the ordinary Roman lived much like the rural population of Italy.

Change in the arts

These mountain climbers are artists who are not interested in making the traditional journey to Rome to paint ruins or copy bas-reliefs. They want to paint nature as it is. The same concern for realism prompted French artists to paint the lifelike movement of horses and the confusion of weapons in great battle scenes. While Jacques Louis David was a great classical artist, he was concerned with realism, too. In his famous *Coronation of Napoleon,* the faces of the Emperor's followers are shown in all their ordinary roughness under elaborate hair styles.

Official architects created works inspired by classical antiquity. But the triumphal arches, churches, and palaces built in the ancient Roman style so admired by Napoleon were not widely popular. People were already becoming fascinated by the Middle Ages and its Romantic style.

The period of the French Revolution and Napoleon's days as First Consul inspired the great German composer Beethoven to dedicate his Third Symphony to Napoleon. However, Beethoven was a true Republican; when Napoleon crowned himself Emperor, he withdrew the dedication.

The two great French writers of the time—one of the leaders of the new Romantic movement in literature, Chateaubriand, and the famous Germaine de Staël—also hated dictatorships and so were exiled from Paris.

Twenty years of war and revolution had profoundly altered people's feelings and taste. The Romantic return to nature is typified by the young German climbers in the picture. They had read the Romantic writers such as Rousseau and Chateaubriand and were ready to change the cold rigidity of Neoclassicism for the color, the adventure, and the love of nature of the new Romanticism.

Budding Romanticism demanded that an artist paint from nature.

Master painters, such as Napoleon's great Neoclassic court painter David, welcomed many young students to their studios. Antoine Jean Gros, an early Romanticist, was David's favorite pupil. To amuse themselves, the art students above duel with paintbrushes.

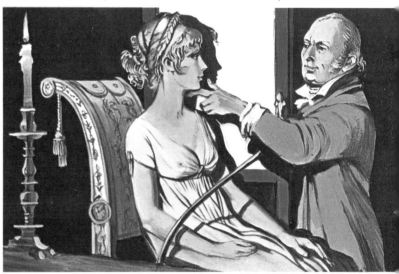

Napoleon loved the French classic drama. So the seventeenth-century playwrights Corneille and Racine regained their popularity, and great actors played in authentic costume, wearing Roman cloaks and helmets. The classical scenery was superb.

An Englishman invented a new way to make portraits without a single error. Using a candle to cast a sharp shadow of his subject's profile on paper, the artist traced the outline with a pencil, then finished by filling it in with a paintbrush.

The court of Princess Pauline Borghese in Milan became a meeting place for musicians. Frequent concerts took place there with the most celebrated singers from the Italian opera house La Scala performing. The audiences appreciated and admired their talent.

STORIES ABOUT ANIMALS

monotreme, does indeed have only one aperture, which serves the digestive, urinary, and genital systems.

The Platypus or Duckbill

Paris/1802

In his *General and Specific History of Reptiles,* the naturalist Daudin devoted several chapters to the gastronomic and therapeutic qualities of frogs and toads. Frog bouillon was recommended to convalescents and people with delicate stomachs. In many European countries green frogs' legs are in demand because they are excellent stewed or fried. In one region, called the Piemonte, the entire animal is eaten after being gutted and cleaned. And what about toads? It is rumored that when the toads gather together to mate in a marshland near Paris, men fish for them with long-handled basket nets. Then they cut off the legs, which they sell in Paris as frogs' legs!

Egypt/1799

General Bonaparte has created a new regiment called the Regiment of the Egyptian Dromedaries. This regiment is made up of four companies, each consisting of 100 men. The soldiers and officers wear uniforms that have been designed in an Oriental style by Kléber, the commander of the Egyptian campaign.

The Regiment of the Dromedaries

Switzerland/1799

When General Brune's troops left Bern, they took many of the city's treasures with them. Among the items they took were emblems of the old Swiss canton picturing a bear, which they attached to their cannon carriages.

France/1800

Two Frenchmen, a father and son by the name of Dubois, have taken up a strange occupation, the cultivation of spiders. In little wooden boxes measuring about 15 centimeters square, they keep more than 10,000 of these "weavers." The spiders are fed flies throughout the summer months and pieces of raw meat during other seasons. The webs spun by the spiders are cut every week with the greatest of care. Then they are spun and woven into pieces of cloth about eight centimeters in length.

England/1802

Some time ago the Royal Zoological Society received from Australia the dried skin of an extraordinary little animal. It had the fur of an otter, the tail of a beaver, and the head of a duck. Because of its bizarre appearance, the Society thought the skin was the work of a practical joker. But much to their embarrassment, they have had to admit they made a mistake. This strange little beast does indeed exist in Australia, where it lives in burrows on river banks. Sir Everad Home, who dissected a specimen, has established that the animal is, in fact, a living fossil, thus upsetting all existing zoological conceptions. This "one-opening animal," or

Réunion/1803

The governor of this French possession has imported enormous snails from Madagascar. They are 22 centimeters long, with shells measuring 12 centimeters. These gastropods may well be the largest in the world. They are said to be effective in the treatment of pulmonary tuberculosis. The governor of Réunion may have imported these snails, known as "achatines," in an attempt to cure his consumptive wife. It is suspected that some of the snails being raised in the gardens of the governor's palace have escaped, and their population flourishes on the island, wreaking havoc on the native crops and vegetation.

Paris/1803

After a most scholarly exchange of views, an illustrious professor at the Museum of Natural History settled a very delicate affair by purchasing an elephant at a fair in Rouen. The elephant is to be a companion for Parkie, the female elephant in the Botanical Gardens, who lost her mate last year. Since the loss of her mate, the poor bereaved beast is reported to have shed "many tears," cried out constantly, and grown continually thinner and thinner. Nothing could be done to distract her from her grief, not even putting a camel in her enclosure to remind her of her native Africa. It is hoped that the new companion might ease some of the sorrow that consumed poor Parkie.

France/1804

A woodcutter named Maréchal, a notorious poacher who lived in the village of Longueville near Méry-sur-Seine, has just been sentenced to forced labor for life for playing "the werewolf trick."

To clear the way for his nocturnal marauding, Maréchal spread a rumor that a werewolf was stalking the region. Many people firmly believed his fable and did not dare go out once night had fallen. This was exactly what Maréchal had hoped for. This way no one would be around to catch him while he was poaching.

One resident of the area, however, was skeptical and wanted to know more about this "beast." He took his shotgun and went to lie in wait for the "werewolf" at the spot where Maréchal had said it usually appeared. Sure enough, suddenly the man saw a hairy monster with the head of a wolf coming toward him. He took aim, fired, and missed. Then to his surprise the animal uncovered its chest, pulled out a shotgun, and pointed it at the

hunter. The hunter rushed to get away but was unable to escape a volley of buckshot that severely wounded his legs. This incredible story soon came to the attention of the police, who began an investigation. Naturally they unmasked Maréchal as the "werewolf." He was brought to court, where the judges, making up for lost time, charged him with many of the unsolved burglaries and thefts committed in the region.

Africa/1806

It was learned that Mungo Park, a Scotsman, was drowned while attempting to reach the mouth of the Niger River. Once before, in 1795, Mr. Park unsuccessfully attempted to explore this unknown river. But, exhausted by illness and suffering from hunger, he was unable to continue the expedition.

Mungo Park—B.N.

Austria/1806

An officer of the French troops, stationed in Schönbrunn following the Austerlitz campaign, gave this account of an astonishing event that he himself had witnessed: "The male Bengal tiger at the Schönbrunn Zoo was usually fed meat from the butcher shop, but when it was ill, it was given live young animals. Their warm blood was supposed to help cure it. Once, when the tiger was ill, they threw him a young dog. At the time, the tiger was crouched, resting its head on its front legs. When the dog recovered from its ini-

tial fright, it approached the tiger and began to lick the tiger's eyes. The tiger found this so soothing that, forgetting his passion for living flesh, he not only spared the animal's life but also showed his appreciation by caressing the dog. The dog continued to lick, and in a few days the tiger was cured. Since then, the two animals have lived together in the most perfect harmony."

Russia/1806

The Russian naturalist Adams has discovered the body of a mammoth. It was the first one to be found. Almost completely preserved in ice, the body of this enormous pachyderm was disengaged from the ice with infinite care and then sent to St. Petersburg.

This remarkable discovery was due to some unusual circumstances. It had been known for a long time that in the warmer season, Samoyeds came to the Iakoute Islands to dig up pieces of ivory that had come from prehistoric animals. However, a fearful legend circulated among the natives that whoever dared to dig an entire animal out of a glacier brought terrible curses upon himself. Then, in 1799, an Iakoute made a discovery. He found a mammoth in a glacier, and it had two enormous ivory tusks! He did not dare to take the animal himself, but how could anyone indefinitely resist the temptation to take the two enormous tusks that stuck out of the ground? In 1804 the man finally came to a decision—at precisely the same time that Adams was making his way to Iakoute. He had heard rumors about the mammoth and wanted to verify the story. In Iakoute he had the good fortune to recover the first complete mammoth preserved in a glacier.

Saint Helena/1810

The Portuguese, who discovered the island of Saint Helena, introduced goats here during the sixteenth century. The goats have proliferated in such large numbers that the thick forests of ebony trees which covered the island have practically disappeared. So, the governor of this island, which today belongs to England, has ordered that all the goats be killed. Unfortunately, this measure comes too late. The rains have washed all the earth on the slopes out to sea, leaving only the sinister, denuded rocks.

Russia/1813

France needed to requisition 40,000 horses for its cavalry within a period of four months in order to carry on the war being waged against the Russian czar. The Comité Central, instituted by the imperial decree of May 17, 1808, had the responsibility of procuring these horses. The 20 members of the committee, along with the inspector generals in charge of horse breeding and other government officials, were soon in despair. They no longer knew how to meet the never-ending, constantly increasing needs of the cavalry. Hastily they gathered together what remained of the old studs and their offspring, which they managed to locate here and there. The Emperor himself, aware of the cavalry's desperate need for quality mounts, donated a large number of his own horses. These were Arabians and Syrians which had been brought from Egypt. They were the pride of his per-

Prussia/1814

"May the flesh of wild horses be sweet to our palates, under the banner of the cross!" This unusual prayer, which western monks added to their benediction before meals, is decidedly a part of the past. At one time in history some of the larger cities of central Europe maintained troops of sharpshooters whose task was to kill the wild horses that devastated the fields. While these cities have long since disbanded the hunting troops, several herds of wild horses still roamed here and there. The majority of them took refuge in the forests of the Duisbourg region. This year several thousand hunters surrounded these herds and virtually wiped them out. At the end of the hunt, no less than 260 horses had been killed, not counting those others that had been wounded or had wandered off and could not be found.

Geneva/1814

Up until this time, it has always been believed that the mating of the queen bee took place in the hive. Francis Huber of Geneva discovered that it actually takes place in the air. Huber is a Swiss naturalist famous for his observations of the honeybee. His discovery is all the more astonishing since he became blind early in his life. Much of his scientific research has been done with the help of his wife and assistants.

After he studied *Notes Relative to the History of Insects* by Ferchault de Réaumur, which had been read to him by his servant, Huber embarked on a series of experiments aided by his servant and an assistant. They carried out Huber's instructions with great care. Huber has created a man-made layered beehive, and has accurately described the nature and origin of beeswax, as well as the methods used by bees to knead and mix the wax plates they use to build the cells of their hives.

A cossack horseman—B.N.

Russia/1813

In the little village of Smorgony, the soldiers of the Grand Army found a place called the Academy of Bears where bears were raised and trained.

sonal stables. Spain and Germany supplied France with additional horses, and these completed the forces. It is feared by many that this lengthy and grueling military campaign might very well lead to the ruin of horse breeding in France, for so many of the well-bred reproducers have already been plundered or killed in the fierce battles in Russia.

Russia/1814

Igor Prokopovitch, a Ukranian beekeeper, has created a new kind of hive with movable frames in which it is possible to move the sections of Huber's hive. A frame of wooden rails supports the layers of wax, which are filled with honey, pollen, and eggs. These can be transferred from one hive to another or replaced by new frames without disturbing the worker bees.

America/1826

Pelican by J.J. Audubon—Usis

In the United States, John James Audubon, who studied painting in France under Jacques Louis David, has begun to publish the first plates of a large album devoted entirely to paintings of birds. These paintings are drawn from life with remarkable precision. When the album is completed, there will be over 400 plates. This work will undoubtedly make its mark on the history of ornithology, following that of Alexander Wilson, who died in 1813 before the ten volumes which he had devoted to the same subject had been published in their entirety.

Owl and Gray Squirrel by J.J. Audubon

France/1815

Napoleon, like any cavalry soldier, needs very dependable horses to ride in battles. Like many generals and leaders, he likes his mounts to be white. He keeps about 60 white horses at the Imperial Horse Farm at Saint-Cloud.

His favorite white horse, Marengo, has carried Napoleon into many battles. He is so well trained that he is not startled by gunfire, animals, or the general chaos of a battle.

This year Marengo was slightly wounded at Waterloo. When the battle was over, though, Marengo was still strong enough for the defeated Napoleon to ride during his escape from the English forces.

General de la Ferriere l'Evesque, called "Peg Leg"
Photo by J. Decker.

Waterloo/June 18, 1815

No doubt in a plan to improve his company's food, a soldier in Napoleon's Imperial Guard shot a pigeon. It was not an ordinary pigeon. When the soldier went to pick it up, he noticed that a message was attached to one of its legs. It was a "spy pigeon" which had been shot as it was flying toward England with important information about the progress of a battle being waged at the time.

This pigeon, and others like it, belong to a group of English financiers. People working with them in Europe write messages about the war and attach them to the birds, who then fly back to their dovecotes in England. The English financiers are the first in their country to get this information. Thanks to the pigeons they are able to successfully speculate at will, using their privileged information.

B.N.   Mr BAUCHER,
Montant son Cheval Partisan.

PALACE GOSSIP

PERFUMES FROM THE ORIENT FOR JOSEPHINE

The sultan of Darfour gave the Emperor a gift of four civet cats, thinking that this gift would greatly honor him. But Napoleon, who probably did not appreciate their odor, had them brought immediately to his wife Josephine at the Château de Malmaison.

Rid us of the wolves

B.N.

It is no secret to the people in the countryside. They know that throughout the land the masters of the wolfhunt do what they can to foster reproduction of wolves so that they can have the pleasure of hunting these predators. Whether or not this is true, it is a fact that the population of wolves multiplied, and not only in France if one is to judge by a leaflet which is being circulated:

"If the Great Napoleon, that Emperor of France, King of Italy, Protector of Germany and Helvetia were to declare, 'There must be no more wolves in Europe,' then these devouring enemies of society would be destroyed!"

Higher praise could not be paid to the Emperor even if the point was missed, for what wolves were they talking about—man or beast?

ANIMALS ON THE FURNITURE

It seems as though the interior decorators of this time are determined to turn elegant dwellings into veritable menageries. From crowing cocks to the Egyptian sphinx, lotus, and scarabs, the designers Percier and Fontaine ornament furniture with an astonishing collection of fanciful and allegoric animals which have probably been copied from the statuary in the gardens of the Château de Malmaison. Eagles and bees have been chosen by the Emperor as his own emblems. Swans, lions, rams, horses, butterflies, griffins, sea horses, and sinister

A mahogany console from the Château de Malmaison
Photo by Lauros-Giraudon

ox skulls decorate table tops, borders, and crosspieces of the furniture.

Roaring lions decorate large, deep armchairs as well as little four-drawered writing tables.

Furniture belonging to Madame Récamier

GREEN UNIFORMS FOR THE HUNTSMEN

General Berthier, the Emperor's aide-de-camp, sent a letter to Talleyrand, the grand chamberlain. It concerned the Emperor's hunting and shooting outfit and the etiquette for wearing it:

. . . I beg you to order that the uniforms of the Emperor's huntsmen be made and worn as follows:

A dragon-green dress coat with a straight collar. The cuffs and pockets should be adorned with metal buttons engraved with different types of game.

A short white jacket and green trousers.

Top boots or leather-buckled gaiters; a sword belt with a very light hunting knife to be worn over the dress coat.

A plain hat

In summer, when the Emperor arrives at a hunt, he will take off his dress coat and will put on a short green cashmere hunting jacket and a round gray hat lined in green.

After the hunt, the Emperor will put his dress coat back on.

All those who are in the Emperor's service or have the honor of accompanying him on hunting and shooting expeditions will be dressed in the same fashion.

Falcons for the imperial hunt

To bring back to the imperial hunts some of the pomp that they had enjoyed during the time of Louis XIII, the Emperor has decided to revive the prestige of falconry. To do this he has engaged two famous Dutch falconers named Daams and Dankers, whom he had brought to Versailles. Four persons are assigned to help them with the falcons.

A PECULIAR HUNTER

A certain Count Boisrot de Lacour, who was the master of the wolf hunt in the area of L'Allier, has contributed a voluminous *Treatise on the Art of Hunting with Hounds* to the existing literature pertaining to the subject. He dedicated this treatise to the duke of Neufchâtel, marshal of the Empire, who was the Emperor's master of the hounds.

There is a question as to whether it was due to a strong desire to please the Emperor or a wish to be a writer that this distinguished hunter exchanged his rifle for a pen, because many elegant embellishments can be found in his work, such as the following:

"Under the pre-Revolutionary regime, a nobleman who loved to hunt would insist upon preserving many destructive animals on his estate.

He soon became hated by everyone around him. He did not care that these animals might justifiably cause annoyance and vexation among his neighbors. He believed that he was only exercising his natural right, even if this infringed upon the personal property of others."

Boisrot de Lacour himself acts differently. In order to keep the "destructive animals" from proliferating, he says, "If I like a region, I buy myself a piece of property, shoot all the game, and when there is no more, I sell the estate and buy myself another one."

MALMAISON ZOOLOGICAL PARK

In her château at Malmaison, Napoleon's first wife, the Empress Josephine, had her gardeners fill large and beautiful gardens with extraordinary plants. After roses, which are her favorite flowers, come tulips, which she has had imported directly from Holland. It is said that she once paid more than 4,000 francs for a single bulb, and that the total bill from her suppliers surpassed 40,000 francs in one year.

The Empress ordered the French minister in London to send her two gentle, well-behaved horses trained to be ridden by women. These were added to the vast stables that she already possesses. Five beautiful merino sheep arrived from Spain, and costumed herdsmen tend a herd of cows which she brought in from Valais. Malmaison has begun to look like a botanical garden and zoological park.

Little horses from the French island of Ouessant gallop on the lawns. In enclosed parks, one can see gazelles, kangaroos, antelopes, a gnu, and even an unusual zebra. These zebras are said to have become so rare in Africa that they are practically extinct. On the little ponds, white and black swans glide along with ducks from China. From all over the world Josephine has been sent parrots, parakeets, cockatoos, pigeons, blackbirds, and a large number of birds that came from the Antilles. The Empress even paid a high price in gold for some storks from Alsace. As for the Emperor, his wife's follies make him laugh. It is said that when he comes to see her, he amuses himself by firing at the swans on the pond from his window, just for the pleasure of irritating her.

Château de Malmaison

Josephine and her attendants inside the greenhouse at Malmaison

A view of the cowshed at Malmaison

Glossary

Agriculture Farming

Architecture The science or art of building

Aristocracy Any class that is considered superior because of birth, culture, or wealth

Armaments War supplies and equipment

Arsenal A place where military weapons and ammunition are stored, manufactured, or repaired

Autonomy Self-government

Bivouac To camp outside, usually without shelter

Brig A square-rigged ship with two masts

Canal A waterway that has been dug through land to provide a means of transportation

Cavalry Soldiers who fight on horseback

Clergy Those who are ordained to do religious work, such as ministers and priests

Conscription The compulsory drafting of men into the army or navy

Coronation A ceremony which is held to crown a king, queen, or emperor

Craftsman A skilled workman

Deport To banish

Dragoon A heavily armed soldier who fought on horseback

Emigrate To move out of one's own country and settle in another

Emperor The ruler of an empire

Espadrilles Casual shoes or sandals with rope soles

Frigate A three-masted sailing warship used in the eighteenth and nineteenth centuries

Gangrene The decay and death of body tissue due to loss of blood supply

Grenadiers Members of a company of soldiers who are the tallest and best in a regiment; also, soldiers who carry and throw grenades

Guerrilla warfare Warfare which uses various small-scale tactics intended to harass and demoralize the enemy

Illiterate Unable to read or write

Industry Any kind of business, trade, or manufacturing

Infantry Soldiers who have been trained, equipped, and organized to fight on foot

Jacobins People who belonged to a radical political group that originated in Paris during the French Revolution

Metallurgy The science or art of working with metals

Monarchy A government headed by a king, queen, or emperor

Nobility Those who are of high birth, title, or rank

Pageantry An elaborate display; pomp

Peasant A farmer of the working class

Philosopher A person who tries to find the truth and studies the principles behind all knowledge

Privateer A privately owned ship that is authorized by a government to attack and capture enemy ships; also, a captain or crew member of such a ship

Resistance An underground movement in a country that is under military control by a foreign power

Revolution A complete overthrow of the ruling government

Royalist One who supports a king or royal government

Sappers Soldiers responsible for constructing trenches and fortifications; also, soldiers whose responsibility is to lay, locate, and disarm mines

Serf A slave who belonged to the land he worked on and who was bought and sold along with the land

Smuggling To illegally and secretly bring something into or take something out of a country

Textile A woven or knit fabric

Tribunal A court of justice

Index

1 2 3 4 5 6 7 8-U-88 87 86 85 84 83